MW00886842

# POODESSA & DUKE

## and a

## Guardian Angel

By Kelly Garrett

Illustrated by Kaieri

Copyright © 2018 Kelly Garrett. All rights reserved.

ISBN : 1729513064
ISBN-13: 978-1729513064

I lovingly dedicate this book to
Caleb & Levi

*Ciao* my little friends.  My name is Poodessa, and this is my pal, my buddy Duke. Oh, "*ciao*" in Italian means both hello *and* goodbye.

Between you and me, I think God put dogs on earth to teach us about love and patience.  I most surely know that's why grandmas were sent from heaven and put on this earth.

I had a wonderful grandma.  She's in heaven now, watching over me.  Her name is
Grandma Luisa Josephine.

My grandma was filled with kindness, faith and goodness.  Oh, how I loved her!

Let's see...you can call her Grandma too.
That way, it's like I am sharing her with you.
She'd like that!

Grandma Luisa had a way of making
everything "all better."


She was always around to offer a good story
or clever saying that kept me on my best behavior.


I still carry and use her warm, loving words of wisdom.
They comfort and guide me even today.


Please allow me and my buddy Duke to share some of
Grandma's quotes with you now.
Go ahead, turn the page.

One of the earliest quotes I can recall from Grandma Luisa is:

# REMEMBER

# TO

A little p.s. - a smile goes a long way.

Another favorite saying from Grandma is:

# SAVE FOR
# A RAINY DAY

Grandma Luisa was big on saving *everything*...

# MANGIA

(Italian for "to eat")

Now Grandma Luisa, *best grandma ever*,
made most things better with a big plate
of her famous spaghetti.  Yum!

For extra love,
be sure to add
a meatball!

Grandma Luisa was always around
to remind me that:

# This Too
# Shall Pass

# THE GOOD LORD WORKS
# IN MYSTERIOUS WAYS

Yep, Grandma would always tell me
the rainbow was God's promise that
there would never be
another flood.


I still look for that beautiful rainbow
after every rain!

# JUST HAVE A LITTLE FAITH

Grandma would always say,

"Faith is like the wind....
You can't see it, *but you can feel it.*"

Be grateful for what you do have...
*like a delizioso (delicious) cannoli.*
Every Wednesday, Grandma Luisa would
bring us this Italian pastry
from her favorite bakery.
What a special treat!

# Wish in One Hand,
# Want in the Other

Grandma, with a
shrug of her shoulders,
would softly say:


# BETTER LAUGHING
# THAN CRYING

# The MORE the MERRIER

Everyone has something to contribute.

Everyone!

And above all, remember that

# IT WILL BE OKAY

Another little p.s. - a hug goes a long way!

One final "*ciao*" to you my little friends.

Be good and I will see you soon!

~Poodessa

# ABOUT THE AUTHOR

## Kelly Garrett

**K**elly was born in Michigan but now calls Atlanta, Georgia, home. Grateful for having such a benevolent grandma, and knowing and understanding the importance of reading, Kelly decided to put the two together.  You are now reading her first effort to do just that-this very children's picture book.  It has been a labor of love for Ms. Garrett.

The hope is yes, to entertain, but more importantly to get children engaged in reading.  Reading aloud stimulates the imagination, expands the understanding of the world, and aids in listening skills and the development of language.  Most importantly, in addition to learning some great life lessons, is the quality of time spent reading together.

Kelly can be reached at poodessa@gmail.com

Other books by Kelly Garrett include:
*Poodessa's Pragmatic Practices* (on amazon)
*Poodessa.com* (coming soon to amazon)

ILLUSTRATOR:  Kaieri

Miss Kaieri went to school at the Art Institute of Pittsburgh.
She has done freelance work for five years.
You can see her creative talents on Fiverr.com.
I can't thank her enough for making Poodessa come to life on these pages.

A special "thank you" to:

My mom for encouraging me to write a children's book

My Creative Director (KG) *who wishes to remain anonymous*

My ℒittle 𝒞ara

Miss Newana Alodia

And of course, Grandma!


In memory of Grandma, proceeds from this book
will go to Kelly's two favorite charities.

(They cannot be listed for legal reasons but are
referenced in *Poodessa's Pragmatic Practices*)

Made in the USA
Columbia, SC
09 November 2021

48595896R00018